# Jobs People Do

# Nurses

by Emily Raij

raintree
a Capstone company — publishers for children

Raintree is an imprint of Capstone Global Library Limited, a company incorporated in England and Wales having its registered office at 264 Banbury Road, Oxford, OX2 7DY – Registered company number: 6695582

www.raintree.co.uk
myorders@raintree.co.uk

Edited by Gena Chester
Designed by Kyle Grenz
Original illustrations © Capstone Global Library Limited 2021
Picture research by Jo Miller
Production by Spencer Rosio
Originated by Capstone Global Library Ltd
Printed and bound in India

978 1 3982 0312 9 (hardback)
978 1 3982 0311 2 (paperback)

**British Library Cataloguing in Publication Data**
A full catalogue record for this book is available from the British Library.

**Acknowledgements**
We would like to thank the following for permission to reproduce photographs:
Shutterstock: Alfonso de Tomas, 23, ALPHA PROD, 11, Creativa Images, 23, Dragana Gordic, 16, Duplass, 17, George Rudy, 7, Image Point Fr, 13, Kzenon, 19, l i g h t p o e t, 10, LightField Studios, 21, michaeljung, 1, MIGUEL G. SAAVEDRA, 23, Minerva Studio, Cover, mirtmirt, 25, Monkey Business Images, 6, 8, 9, 18, New Africa, 27, Olesia Bilkei, 15, Prachaya Roekdeethaweesab, 8, Rob Marmion, 5, XiXinXing, 20

# Contents

Words in **bold** are in the glossary.

# What is a nurse?

Nurses care for people. They treat sick **patients**. Nurses also keep people healthy. They help children and adults.

You sometimes see a nurse at your **check-ups**. They measure height and weight. Some give hearing and eye tests. Nurses sometimes give injections.

Patients may have health questions. Nurses can give some answers. They talk to patients and their families. Nurses put patient information into a patient's file.

Then nurses talk to a doctor. The doctor may ask the nurse to do other tests. Nurses and doctors are a team. They care for people together.

# Where nurses work

Nurses work in many places. Some work in **clinics** and **hospitals**. Others work in doctor's surgeries. A nurse can care for people at home. Some nurses work at military bases. They may care for soldiers.

Some nurses do **research**. They may work in **labs**. Companies pay them. Governments can pay them too.

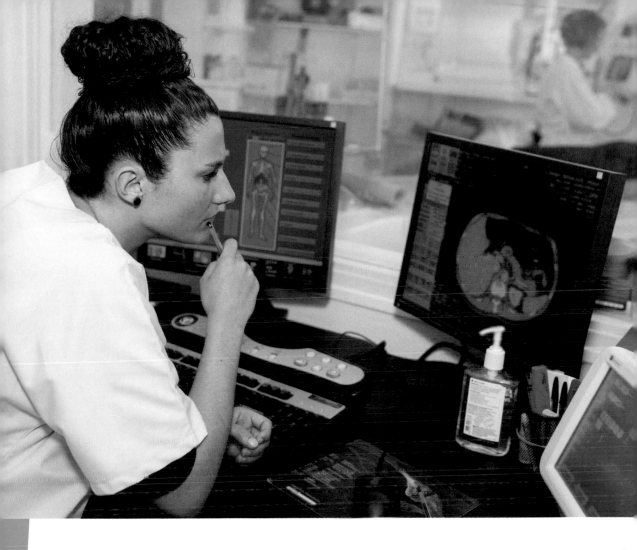

Other nurses study diseases at teaching hospitals. They do tests. Some use special tools. They treat patients to see what works best. These nurses make health care better.

Nurses work at some schools too. Pupils go to nurses if they get hurt. Nurses treat sick pupils. Some pupils have to take medicine. School nurses give it to them.

School nurses also teach about healthy choices. They talk to pupils about eating well. They also talk about getting enough sleep and exercise.

# Types of nurses

There are many types of nurses. They care for all groups of people.

Some treat children. Others treat only adults or look after the elderly. There are nurses who care for babies. These nurses also take care of mums who have just given birth. A **midwife** is a nurse who cares for pregnant women. This nurse helps with births.

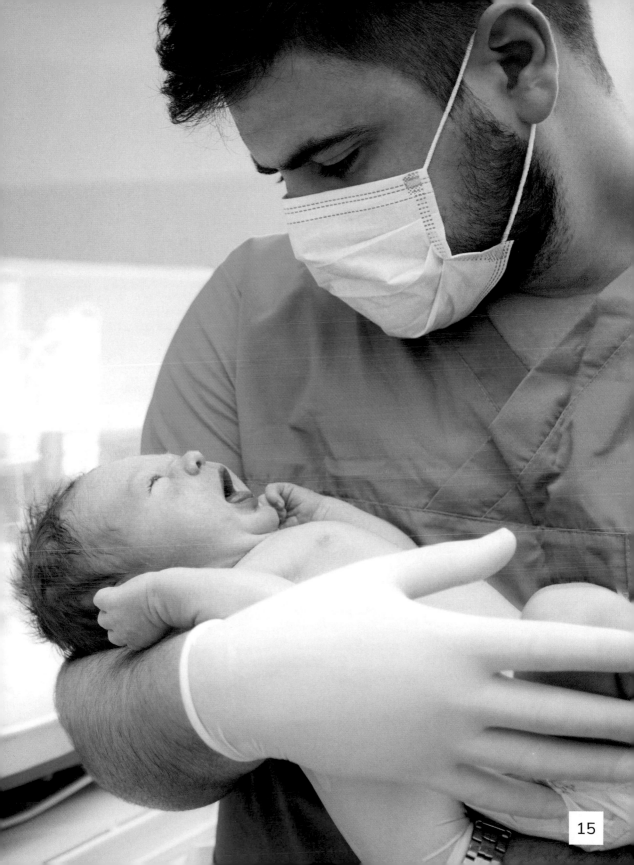

Some nurses help with simple care. They bathe patients. They clean cuts and change bandages. These nurses check for signs of good health. This includes breathing and heart rates.

A nurse checking her patient's health

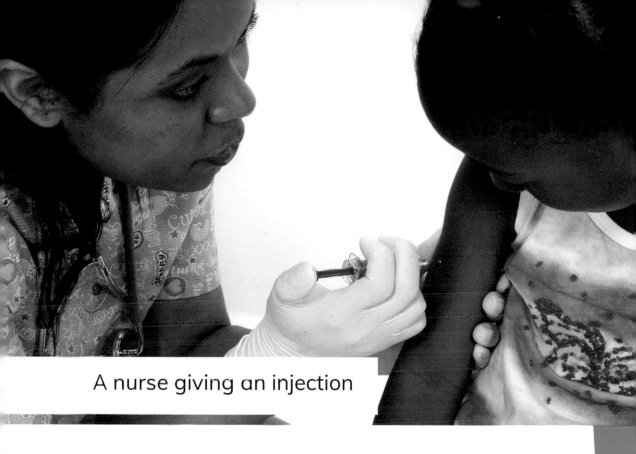

A nurse giving an injection

Other nurses have more training. They help in other ways. They give out some medicines. They also give injections and take blood for testing.

Higher-level nurses can run medical tests on patients and **prescribe** medicine. They treat injuries and illnesses.

# What nurses do

Nurses do many things. Some help before operations. They may get the patient ready for the operation. Other nurses help during the operation. They hand the doctor tools. Some care for patients after their operations.

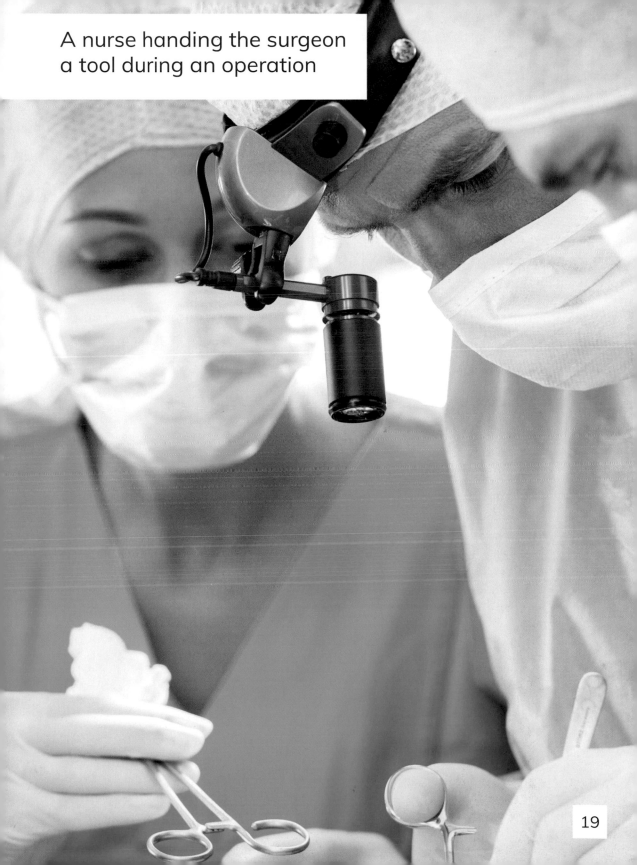

A nurse handing the surgeon a tool during an operation

Some nurses teach about care. They may teach students. But they also talk to families. They tell parents about a child's illness. They go over what will happen to the child during **treatment**.

Nurses work with a team. Teams are led by doctors. They come up with a care plan. Sometimes they change the plan. They might try a new treatment.

Most nurses work long days. They may work 10 to 12 hours a day. They work three to four days a week. Nurses are on their feet a lot. Comfy shoes help!

Nurses sometimes wear **scrubs**. The trousers and top can be washed with strong soap to kill germs. Scrubs let others know who nurses are. They can tell what area they work in.

Nurses wash their hands to kill germs. They wear gloves. This keeps patients healthy. It also stops nurses from getting ill.

# Nurses' tools

scrubs

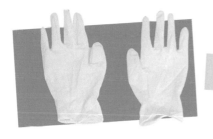

gloves

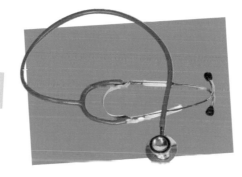

stethoscope

watch

shoes

# How to become a nurse

Nurses have to study for a degree in nursing. It helps to have studied science at A level. Students need to decide what type of nursing they want to do – for example, be a nurse for adults or a nurse for children.

Nurses study at **university** for three or four years. Part of the degree involves spending time working in hospitals or clinics to gain practical experience.

Once they have their degree, some nurses train in a special area of nursing care. Midwives must do this. So must nurses who want to care for cancer patients.

These nurses study and take tests in their area.

Sometimes you can become a nurse by being an apprentice and working and studying at the same time.

# Famous nurses

Nurses help people around the world. Florence Nightingale was a nurse in the 1800s. She cared for soldiers during the Crimean War. She made sure hospitals were clean. She also started a nursing school.

Edith Cavell was a British nurse. She cared for soldiers during the First World War. She also helped around 200 British, French and Belgian soldiers escape from the Germans.

**Florence Nightingale**

# Fast facts

- **What nurses do:**
They care for people and help doctors treat patients.

- **Where nurses work:**
doctors' surgeries, clinics, hospitals and schools

- **Key tools and clothing:**
gloves, scrubs, comfy shoes, thermometer

- **Education needed:**
A levels (usually at least one science), degree in nursing

- **Famous nurses:**
Florence Nightingale, Edith Cavell

# Glossary

**check-up**  visit to the doctor's to see if a person is healthy

**clinic**  building where people go to get medical care; some doctors have surgeries in clinics

**hospital**  building where doctors and nurses care for people who are ill or injured

**lab**  place where experiments or tests are done

**midwife**  person who helps women give birth

**patient**  person who gets medical care

**prescribe**  order a medicine

**research**  study and learn about a subject

**scrubs**  loose, lightweight uniform worn by workers in clinics and hospitals

**treatment**  way to heal, cure or control symptoms of illness